PLANTS

A SCIENCE ACTIVITY BOOK

BY
PAT AND BARBARA WARD

COPYRIGHT © 1998 Mark Twain Media, Inc.

ISBN 10-digit: 1-58037-066-7
      13-digit: 978-1-58037-066-0

Printing No. CD-1304
Mark Twain Media, Inc., Publishers
Distributed by Carson-Dellosa Publishing Company, Inc.

Table of Contents

Introduction

Good day! I am your new tour guide, and I would like for you to come with me for a while; we are going to do some traveling. I work for a special travel agency, so you will not need any money or luggage for this trip! The only thing you'll need is your imagination. If you are ready, then let's go.

Be sure you have fastened your seatbelt. We will be moving along very quickly. We are already at our first stop: southern Texas in late February. Look around you. You will see prickly pear cactus, little bluestem and Indian grasses, and mesquite trees. Palm trees and live oaks raise their branches toward the sky, while the bluebonnets and Indian paintbrush begin to bloom below.

If you have had a good look around, it is time to move along to our next stop. This time we are going to central Illinois in April. Now you will see spring beauties covering the ground in lawns, while trillium and Dutchman's britches bloom in wooded areas. Redbud and crabapple trees show off their lovely blooms, and yellow daffodils welcome the warmer weather. Corn and bean crops are starting to grow in the farmers' fields.

Take one last look, as it is time to move on to our third stop: western Kansas in June. This time you will be seeing large fields of winter wheat in its greenest glory. Coneflowers, butterfly weeds, and shooting stars dazzle us on the rolling hill prairies. Fremont cotton-woods and willow trees grow along the sides of creeks. Thickets of wild plum, sassafras, and fragrant sumac are pleasing not only to the eyes, but to the noses as well. We cannot stay too long, so enjoy the view while you can.

For our next stop, we will head to northern Minnesota in September. Swamp red maples are turning bright red, along with the sumacs. Orange-colored sugar maples and yellow paper birches are a pleasant sight. Jack pines, Canadian hemlock, white cedar, and black spruce maintain their lovely green needles almost all year. Blue and white asters are finishing up their lovely display of color. Mosses and lichens are getting ready for the colder winter months ahead.

Our final stop moves us indoors to a living room in December. You will notice poinsettias, a Christmas tree, Christmas cactus, some ferns, and ivy decorating the room. Now our journey is over, and it is time to go back home. Thank you for your attention and cooperation during this trip. We hope you will travel with us again.

Welcome back! As you probably realize, the main attraction of our trip was plants. Plants grow almost everywhere! They come in many colors, shapes, and sizes. They grow and bloom at different times of the year in different places around this country and around the world. Some plants are beneficial, and other plants are harmful. Sometimes we just enjoy the beauty of plants, and other times we use the plants to improve our lives. Let's see just how much we can learn about plants.

Name _____ Date _____

For the student:

1. What are five common plants in your area for each season of the year?

_____

_____

_____

_____

2. Think of the colors of the rainbow. (ROY G. BIV) What are some plants which bloom with those colors?

_____

_____

_____

_____

3. What is a common crop plant for your area?

_____

4. What is a beneficial plant for your area?

_____

5. What is a harmful plant for your area?

_____

6. What plants do you have in your classroom?

_____

_____

_____

A Plant by Any Other Name

We want to learn as much as we can about plants. First, we must decide just what a plant is. Let's work on a good definition for the word *plant*.

Scientists have studied many living and nonliving things. They call all of the living things **organisms**. They have identified six characteristics that are true for all organisms. These characteristics are known as the six features of life.

1. Organisms reproduce.
2. Organisms grow.
3. Organisms develop.
4. Organisms use energy.
5. Organisms need food.
6. Organisms are made of cells.

Think about plants. Do they fit these six characteristics? Yes, they sure do. Let's see how.

1. Plants reproduce.

Spider flowers, or cleome, make seeds. In the fall, when the flowers begin to fade, the seeds fall to the ground. They stay there during the winter months and then germinate, sprout, and grow the next spring. New cleome flowers will show off their lovely blooms the following summer. The cleome have reproduced.

2. Plants grow.

Oak trees start their lives as tiny acorns. When the temperature, moisture, and soil conditions are just right, the acorn will begin to grow. After many years, the tiny acorn becomes a large, majestic oak tree. The acorn has grown.

3. Plants develop.

Corn begins as a small seed planted in the ground. When it begins to grow, two tiny leaves emerge from the seed. They reach up toward the sun and make food for the tiny plant. As the corn grows, it adds more leaves, and the stalk becomes thicker and stronger. A tassel forms, and the plant is pollinated by insects or the wind blowing through the area. Finally an ear of corn forms, protected by the corn husk and silk. The corn has developed from a seed into a mature plant.

4. Plants use energy.

Plants make their own food. They must use energy from the Sun to combine carbon dioxide and water, making food and oxygen. Without the energy from the Sun, the plants would not be able to make their food, so they could not survive.

5. Plants need food.

Just like we need food to give us energy to work and play, plants need energy to grow and reproduce. Plants get some energy from the Sun and more energy from the food they make themselves. Without food, plants cannot survive.

6. Plants are made of cells.

If you look at a thin piece of plant under a microscope, you will see that a plant is made of many tiny cells. The cells have many important parts that help keep the plant alive and growing.

Now we have the beginning of our definition. **Plants are organisms.** When scientists have identified organisms, they study the structures of those organisms. They look at many characteristics, such as the number of **cells**, the presence of a **nucleus**, the presence of **cell walls**, and the types of other structures, or **organelles**, within a cell.

Plants are multicellular organisms. They have more than one cell. Their cells work together to help the plants with all of their life functions. Plant cells have a nucleus, which controls the many life activities of each plant. They also have cell walls, which provide protection and support for the plants as they live and grow. Finally, plants have cell organelles. These are structures that help each plant's nucleus do its many jobs.

Now we can improve our definition. **Plants are multicellular organisms that contain nuclei and cell walls, as well as cell organelles.**

There is one more thing that we need to think about to help us finish up our definition. Scientists like to consider how organisms get their food. Plants are special because they are able to make their own food in a process called **photosynthesis**. Because most plants can make up their own food, scientists classify them as **producers**.

Now we can finish up our definition. **Plants are multicellular organisms that contain nuclei and cell walls, as well as cell organelles, allowing them to carry on life processes as producers.**

Here's an interesting fact or two:

Cacti are only found in American deserts.
The tallest kind of cactus is the saguaros.
It can grow to 15 meters in height.
(That's about 50 feet!)
It can weigh up to seven tons!
It can be up to 200 years old!

Name_____ Date _____

For the student:

1. What are the six features of life?

_____

_____

_____

_____

2. Are plants considered to be organisms? Why or why not?

_____

_____

_____

3. Bacteria are made of one cell. Are they plants? Why or why not?

_____

_____

_____

4. Why does every plant cell have a nucleus?

_____

_____

_____

5. What other structures do plant cells have?

_____

_____

_____

6. What is a good definition for the word *plant*?

_____

_____

_____

Kings Play Cards On Fridays, Generally Speaking: Classifying Organisms

Scientists love to classify, or put things into groups. All organisms have been divided into five large groups called **kingdoms**. The kingdoms are then divided into smaller groups called **phyla**. The phyla are then divided into smaller groups called **classes**. Classes are divided into **orders** and then into **families**. The next smallest group is called a **genus**, and the smallest group of all is called a **species**. (If you look at the first letter of each of the classifications, you will notice they are the same as the first letters of the words in the title sentence. It is a good way to remember the order of the classification scheme!)

One of the five kingdoms of organisms is the **plant kingdom**. The plant kingdom contains all the plants in the world. There are more than 285,000 different kinds of plants, and scientists are still finding more of them all the time! That's a lot of plants to try to learn and study.

The plant kingdom is divided into two major phyla. The first phylum is the **Bryophyta**, or **nonvascular plants**. Bryophytes include about 22,000 kinds of plants. These plants do not have true roots, stems, or leaves. They do not have tube-like structures to move food and water through them. The smallest bryophytes can only be seen with a microscope, and the largest ones are about 30 centimeters (12 inches) long. Most bryophytes, however, are between 1.2 and 5 centimeters (0.5 and 2 inches) long. Because they do not have any tubes for moving water, most bryophytes are found in moist areas. Some of them, however, have adapted to live in deserts. Mosses, liverworts, and hornworts are all examples of nonvascular plants.

The second plant phylum is the **Tracheophyta**, or **vascular plants**. These plants have tube-like structures inside of them that can move food, water, and minerals to the leaves, stems, and other parts of the plant. Tracheophytes include ferns, "naked seed" plants, and flowering plants. These are some of the most familiar plants, such as pine trees, roses, and tomatoes. Tracheophytes vary in size, from tiny plants to huge redwood trees that grow more than 100 meters (330 feet) tall. Tracheophytes do not need as much direct contact with water as bryophytes do, so they are able to grow in almost every kind of environment.

Here's an interesting fact or two:

Rice is the only grass that will grow completely under water.
Rice is the main food for more than half of the world's population.
Ninety percent of the world's rice is grown in Asia.

     6

Name _____ Date _____

For the student:

1. What do the first letters of the words in the following sentence represent?
 King Phillip comes of fairly good stock.

_____

_____

_____

2. What is the largest group of plants called?

_____

3. What are the two major phyla of plants?

_____

4. How are vascular plants different from nonvascular plants?

_____

_____

5. Why do mosses grow in moist areas?

_____

_____

Activity:

Observing the movement of water through a celery stalk

  Gather several stalks of celery, different colors of food dye, and several small jars of water. Cut a thin slice off the top of each stalk of celery, being careful not to cut off the leaves; then cut off the bottoms of the stalks. Observe the celery and record your observations.

  Label each of the jars with numbers or letters. Put some water in each of the small jars. Vary the amount and temperature of the water. Record the amount and temperature of the water. Dissolve food coloring in the water. Vary the amount and color of food coloring in the jars. Record the amount of food coloring and the color. Place a stalk of celery in each jar and wait 24 hours. At the end of the 24-hour period, observe the celery. Record your observations. Discuss the following questions:

- How does the food dye move through the stalks of celery?
- Is celery a bryophyte or a tracheophyte? Why?
- Does the amount of water affect the final results?
- Does the temperature of the water affect the final results?
- Does the amount of food dye affect the final results?
- Does the color of the food dye affect the final results?

A Class Act

In the previous lesson, you have learned that all organisms are divided into five kingdoms. Plants are classified by scientists into the plant kingdom. Scientists then divide all the plants into two phyla: bryophytes and tracheophytes. Remember that bryophytes are nonvascular plants and tracheophytes are vascular plants. Let's take a look now at the major classes within each of the plant kingdom phyla.

Bryophytes: Musci, Anthocerotae, and Hepaticae

Bryophytes are divided into three classes: **Musci**, which are mosses; **Anthocerotae**, which are hornworts; and **Hepaticae**, which are liverworts.

Mosses, or Musci, are small plants that are able to grow on rocks, tree bark, and in soil. They may also be found in bogs and streams. Mosses prefer moist, shaded areas. If you take a close look at moss, you will notice a thin stalk and small, leaf-like structures. Mosses do not have true stems or leaves. They are not able to move water from one part of the plant to another through tubes. Instead, water must move from one part of the plant to another by a process called **diffusion**. Diffusion can be defined as the process of moving from an area with many molecules to an area with fewer molecules. Diffusion is a very slow process, so mosses never grow very big. Water cannot move fast enough by diffusion to be able to get to all the parts of a big plant. Mosses also do not have roots. They are able to hold onto the rocks, tree bark, and soil by using **rhizoids**. Rhizoids are thin, thread-like structures that grow out of the base of the stalk. Mosses play an important role in nature. They have chemicals in their rhizoids that break down rocks into tiny particles of soil. After many years, mosses help form new soil from the rocks to which they have been attached.

Liverworts are another class of bryophyte. Like mosses, liverworts prefer to live in moist areas. Some liverworts grow on land, while others grow in water. They do not have true stems or leaves either. Liverworts are identified by their flat, ribbon-like shapes. They also move water through them by the process of diffusion. Marchantia is one kind of liverwort. It has dull green, rounded leaf-like structures and prefers to grow close to the ground. Marchantia will grow umbrella-like structures that are called spores. These are the reproductive parts of the liverwort. (Remember, all organisms reproduce!) This plant may be found growing on the floor of a forest or in a terrarium.

Tracheophytes: Filicineae, Gymnospermae, Angiospermae

Tracheophytes are divided into three classes as well: **Filicineae**, or ferns; **Gymnospermae**, or "naked seed" plants; and **Angiospermae**, or flowering plants. Let's take a closer look at these plants, too.

Ferns, or Filicineae, are vascular plants, which means they have tube-like structures that move food and water from one part of the plant to another. Water is able to move rather quickly, so ferns can grow much bigger than mosses or liverworts. Ferns grow in many different places, however, they

prefer soil and air that are moist. There are a great number of ferns that grow in the tropics. They are also commonly found in damp forest areas. Ferns reproduce by spores. If you look on the bottom of fern leaves, or fronds, you may see small, dot-like structures. They are the spore cases. When the spore cases burst open, tiny spores are released. They will become new ferns. Young ferns are often called **fiddleheads** because of their unusual shape. Fern fronds unfurl from fiddleheads and form beautiful new fern plants.

Gymnospermae, or "naked seed" plants, have true leaves, stems, and roots. They have tubes to carry food and water to all parts of the plant. They reproduce by making seeds. Gymnospermae are called "naked seed" plants because their seeds are not formed inside a fruit. Many gymnosperm plants are called **conifers** because they produce their seeds inside of cones. Their leaves may look like needles, and they are often known as evergreen plants because they do not lose all of their leaves at one time. Redwood trees, the tallest and oldest trees known in the world, are gymnosperms. Not all gymnosperms are coniferous or evergreen, however. Ginkgo trees are **deciduous**, meaning they lose all of their leaves in the fall of the year. Gymnosperms grow in a number of places. They can be found in huge evergreen forests, and they can be found as decorative plants in the lawns of homes and businesses. They are important to the lumber and paper industry because they are fast-growing plants. They are not only beautiful plants, but they can be great windbreaks as well.

Finally, Angiospermae, or flowering plants, are plants with true leaves, stems, and roots. They also have a vascular system, or tubes, to carry water and food to all of the parts of the plant. This is a very large group, which contains more than half of all the plants in the world! They reproduce by making seeds inside of fruits. People eat the fruits of many of the angiosperms, such as bananas and tomatoes. Some of the flowers and fruit we do not even notice. Most deciduous trees, such as maples, oaks, and elms, flower in the spring. The flowers may be the same color as the leaves, so we do not always notice them. Angiosperms also provide important raw materials such as lumber. They may be used to beautify lawns and parks. In the fall, people may travel many miles to see the wonderful display of color created when deciduous angiosperms begin to lose their leaves.

Here's an interesting fact or two:

Baobab trees grow in Africa.
They have enormous trunks but very short branches.
They look like they are upside down!
The trunks are often hollow and may be used as bus stops or even for homes.

Name _____ Date _____

For the student:

Read each sentence below. Decide if the sentence is true or false. If the sentence is true, write T on the blank in front of the sentence. If the sentence is false, write F on the blank <u>and</u> change a word or some of the words in the sentence to make it true.

_____ 1. All organisms are divided into five families.

_____

_____ 2. All plants are vascular.

_____

_____ 3. Mosses have rhizoids.

_____

_____ 4. Water moves through bryophytes by the process of diffusion.

_____

_____ 5. Liverworts reproduce with seeds.

_____

_____ 6. Liverworts and mosses are larger than ferns.

_____

_____ 7. Ferns prefer to live in hot, dry areas.

_____

_____ 8. Gymnosperms have true leaves, stems, and roots.

_____

_____ 9. Conifers produce their seeds inside of fruits.

_____

_____ 10. Most of the plants that are living today are angiosperms.

_____

_____ 11. A white pine tree is a flowering plant.

_____

_____ 12. A banana grows from part of a flower.

_____

_____ 13. A tomato plant is an angiosperm.

_____

_____ 14. A maple tree has flowers.

_____

_____ 15. A ginkgo tree is an angiosperm.

_____

Activities:

Identifying ferns, gymnosperms, and angiosperms

1. Tour the school yard or visit a local nursery. Identify the plants you see as ferns, gymnosperms, and angiosperms. Determine which group has the greatest number or variety of plants.

2. Develop a photo library of plants. (Magazines are good sources.) Have students classify the plants by phylum and class.

3. Gather a variety of cones, nuts, and fruits. Find the seeds. Examine the seeds, being sure to record your observations. Identify the adult plants that produce each of the seeds. Determine where the adult plants grow. How many of the plants are grown locally? How many of the fruits and nuts must be brought in from another area?

Here's an interesting fact or two:

There are about 10,000 different kinds of grasses.
Most of them have hollow stems.
Grasses are angiosperms, so they have flowers.
Grasses are pollinated by the blowing winds,
so the flowers do not need to be brightly colored to attract insects.

Pieces of the Puzzle: Parts of a Plant, Parts of a Plant Cell

As we have already learned, plants are organisms. All organisms are made of cells. Let's take a look at what is found in a plant cell.

The **cell** is the smallest part of any plant. The cell is the basic unit of life for every plant. It is the smallest unit that can carry on life processes for a plant. There are some important parts of a cell that you should know.

One of the important structures in a plant cell is the **cell wall**. It provides support and protection for the cell. The cell wall contains a chemical called **cellulose** that helps make the cell strong. It also has waxes that help the cell keep the right amount of water. Animal cells do not have cell walls; plant cells do.

Plant cells also have **protoplast**. That is the living matter inside of a cell. It is surrounded by a **cell membrane**. The protoplast contains **cytoplasm**. You will find other cell structures, such as **vacuoles** and **chloroplasts**, in the cytoplasm.

Vacuoles are tiny structures in plant cells. They hold cell sap. Cell sap consists of sugars, waters, salts, and other chemicals. Animal cells do not have vacuoles, but plant cells do.

Chloroplasts are also special structures that are in plant cells but not in animal cells. These chloroplasts contain chlorophyll and carotenoids, which are very important for the process that plants use to make their own food: photosynthesis. Again, these cell structures are not found in animal cells.

Plant cells have **mitochondria**. These structures are important in the process of **respiration**. Both plant and animal cells must be able to combine food and oxygen in order to release energy. Mitochondria play an important role in the combination of the food and oxygen and in the release of energy.

Finally, each plant cell has a **nucleus**. The nucleus is the control center of the cell. It controls all of the life activities of the cell. It coordinates the activities of all of the other structures in the cell.

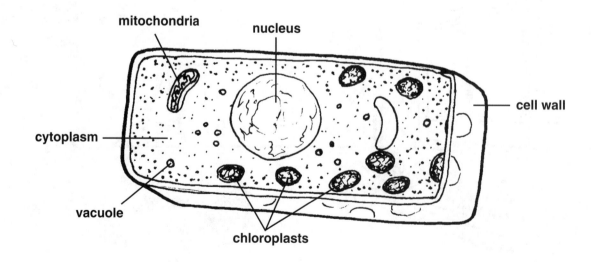

Name _____ Date _____

For the student:

1. What is the smallest part of any plant?

_____

2. What is the function of a cell wall? _____

_____

the vacuoles? _____

the chloroplasts? _____

the mitochondria? _____

the nucleus? _____

3. In what ways are plant cells different from animal cells?

_____

_____

_____

4. In what ways are plant cells the same as animal cells?

_____

_____

_____

Activities:

Observing plant and animal cells

1. Obtain slides of plant cells. Using a microscope, study the plant cells. Draw what you observe in the microscope. If possible, label the parts of the cell.

2. Obtain slides of animal cells. Using a microscope, compare and contrast the plant and animal cell slides. Draw what you observe. Label the parts of the cells that are similar using a pen or marker of one color. Label the parts of the cells that are different using another color pen or marker.

13

Pieces of the Puzzle: Parts of a Plant, Getting to the Root of the Problem

Roots are an important part of a plant. Along with the stem and leaves, roots form the **vegetative matter** in a plant. The roots grow down, with the force of gravity, and they are usually found underground. Some land plants have as many roots under the ground as they have stems, branches, and leaves above the ground. The sizes of roots vary from plant to plant and from area to area.

Roots have three important jobs to do for plants. First, roots hold the plant in the ground. They anchor the plant in the soil so that wind and water will not be able to move the plant easily. Roots also absorb water and minerals that plants need to survive. Special kinds of cells in the roots allow the plant to move water from the roots to the other parts of the plant. Plant parts use the minerals and water to make the food they need to perform all of their life activities. Finally, roots can store food for the plant to use later. Beets, carrots, radishes, and sweet potatoes are examples of plants that store food in their roots.

There are two basic types of roots. The first kind of root is called a **fibrous root**. A good example of a fibrous root could be found if you pulled up some grass. There are many roots attached to the plant, and most of them are about the same size. The roots spread out through the soil to anchor the plant well. The second kind of root is called a **taproot**. If you pulled up a radish, you would have a good example of a taproot. You will notice only one large root, and you should see that it has grown straight down into the soil.

When a root grows out from a seed, it is known as a **primary root**. As the plant continues to grow, it may develop **secondary roots**, which are smaller branches growing off of the primary root. Each root is protected by a **root cap**. It covers the tip of the root to protect it as the root moves through the soil. Many roots will also develop **root hairs**. They are tiny roots that will almost never be more than half an inch long. The root hairs are responsible for absorbing most of the water and minerals. A healthy plant needs plenty of water and minerals to grow, so it may develop many root hairs.

Not all plants grow in soil. Some plants live in water. Their roots often float freely in the water. These roots are still responsible for absorbing the water and minerals that the plant needs. Of course, they are not responsible for anchoring the plant.

Some terrestrial plants do not set their roots in soil either. Some of them attach their roots to other plants, such as trees. The roots absorb water and minerals from the atmosphere and from the host tree. Instead of anchoring into the ground, these roots anchor the plant to the host tree.

Two factors affect plant roots. The first factor is gravity. Roots will grow down with the force of gravity. The second factor is water. Roots will grow toward water. Sometimes that can be a problem in a town with water and sewer lines. If there is a small leak in the water or sewer line, the roots of plants such as trees will begin to grow toward the leaking water. They may grow right into the area with the water and sewer lines, causing problems for the home owners!

Name _____ Date _____

For the student:

1. What three parts of a plant are known as the vegetative matter?

_____

_____

2. What are the three main jobs of roots?

_____

_____

3. What are two basic kinds of roots?

_____

_____

4. What is the difference between a primary root and a secondary root?

_____

_____

5. Why do roots need root caps?

_____

_____

6. Why do some plants have a lot of root hairs?

_____

_____

7. How does gravity affect plant roots?

_____

_____

8. How does water affect plant roots?

_____

_____

Name _____ Date _____

Activities:

Demonstrating that roots take water from the soil for plants

Obtain two matching plants; coleus plants work well. Observe the plants and document your observations. Pot the plants in matching pots in similar soil. Place each of the plants in a holding tray. Attach a plastic bag to the stem of one plant, taping the bag all around the stem and letting it drape over the pot. Develop a watering schedule for the plants. When watering the plant with the plastic bag, water only the leaves and stem. Do not water the soil under the bag. Apply a similar amount of water to the soil of the other plant. Be sure to drain any excess water out of both holding trays. Observe the plants for one week. After one week, compare the two plants.

1. Do the plants look the same at the end of the week? _____

_____

2. Do plants need water to live? _____

_____

3. Where do plants absorb the water they need to stay alive? _____

_____

Demonstrating that roots anchor a plant

Grow two radishes in separate pots. When the plants have grown for about four to five weeks, uproot one of the radishes. Cut off the root about 1/4 inch below the spot where it entered the soil. Replant the radish. Place both radishes in front of a fan. Turn on the fan and observe the plants.

1. Do both plants remain standing? _____

_____

2. What holds a plant in the soil? _____

_____

Name _____ Date _____

Demonstrating that gravity affects root growth

Grow corn seedlings for approximately two weeks. Carefully wrap cotton around three seedlings. Place the cotton and seedlings in three separate test tubes. Using an eyedropper, thoroughly moisten the cotton in each test tube. Tape the three test tubes to a piece of heavy cardboard. One test tube should be taped in a horizontal position, a second test tube should be taped with the seedling upright, and the final one with the seedling placed upside down. Place the cardboard in a spot where it will not be disturbed. Keep the cotton moist. Observe the seedlings for five to seven days. Record your observations.

1. How did the roots grow? _____

_____

_____

2. How did the seedling plants grow? _____

_____

_____

3. What caused the roots to grow down?_____

_____

_____

Observing root growth in different types of soil

Make root-viewing boxes using clean, empty milk cartons. Cut away one side of the milk carton. Insert a plastic bag into the milk carton and fill it with soil. Use a different kind of soil for each viewing box: potting soil, peat moss, sand, gravel, school-yard soil, and so forth. Soak seeds overnight and then add them to the various kinds of soil. Provide adequate water. Observe growth of the plants and roots. Record your observations.

Here's an interesting fact or two:

There are about 80,000 plants that can be eaten.
Right now, most people in the world depend on about 20 plants.
Scientists are finding more food plants that may become important in the future.

Pieces of the Puzzle: Parts of a Plant, What's Holding Things Up? Stems

The stem is another important part of a plant. Stems are usually found above the ground, and they may vary greatly in appearance. Think about redwood trees. The trunks, branches, and twigs of the mighty trees are all considered part of the trees' stems. Think also of a cabbage plant. Beneath the piles of leaves, a short stem barely peeks out of the ground. In general, stems grow up, against the force of gravity. (Remember that roots grow down with the force of gravity.)

Stems have three general jobs to do for a plant. First of all, they hold the leaves up where they can get lots of sunlight. While holding the leaves up, the stem also holds the leaves apart so they can all get their fair share of the sunlight.

Stems have another job, which is to store food and water. Cactus plants may go for long periods of time without getting any rain. They store their water in their stems. Deciduous trees must survive the winter without any new food. Food made during the previous spring and summer can be stored in the trunk of the tree to be used during the cold winter months.

Finally, stems have a third job, which is perhaps their most important. Stems transport food and water between the leaves and roots of the plant. Remember that roots are responsible for absorbing the water that the plant will need to survive. The water must move from the roots to the other parts of the plant. The stem provides the pipeline to move the water. Leaves are responsible for making the plant's food. The food must be able to move to the other parts of the plant that need it. The stem provides the pipelines to move the food as well.

Stems contain three basic types of tissue. **Xylem** tissue is responsible for moving water up from the roots to the other parts of the plant. **Phloem** tissue is responsible for moving food down from the leaves to the other parts of the plants. The third type of tissue is called **cambium**. This is the growth tissue that makes new xylem and phloem as the plant continues to grow.

There are two types of stems in plants. One kind of stem is soft, smooth, and usually green. Plants with this kind of stem are called **herbaceous plants**. These stems can be bent because they do not have a lot of xylem tissue in them. The xylem and phloem tissues in herbaceous plants are found in bundles in the stems. These plants live for only one year or one growing season, and then they die. They are called **annual plants**.

The other kind of stem is rough, woody, and usually a brownish color. Plants with this kind of stem are called **woody plants**. These woody plants include trees and shrubs. These plants can live for many years. They are called **perennial plants**. The xylem and phloem tissues in perennial plants form rings around the stems. Each year another layer of xylem and phloem is made for the plant. The older layers form **growth rings**, one for every year that the plant has been alive. By counting the growth rings on a perennial plant, such as a tree, an observer can determine not only how old the tree is, but what the weather was like during its lifetime. In years with plenty of rain, the growth ring will be thick. In years with lighter rains, the growth ring will be narrow.

When we think of stems, we usually think of stems that grow straight up above the ground. These are called **aerial stems**. However, some aerial stems do not grow straight up. Sometimes stems grow along the ground and are called **runners**. Some kinds of grasses and most strawberries have stems that are runners. When the runners touch the ground, new roots may grow, starting new grass clumps or new strawberry plants.

Not all stems are aerial, however. Some stems are **subterranean**, meaning they grow beneath the ground. **Bulbs**, such as tulips, are actually stems that are surrounded by many leaves. They grow beneath the ground, sending up new leaves and flowers for us to enjoy in the spring. Lily of the Valley stems are also subterranean. They are called **rhizomes**. They grow away from the root beneath the ground. New leaves and flowers will pop up close to the original plants, allowing Lily of the Valley to fill in an area rather quickly. Sometimes rhizomes swell up beneath the ground. They are called **tubers**. Tubers store energy for use later on. Potatoes are examples of stems that grow beneath the ground. Potatoes are tubers.

Other stems have special adaptations that allow them to live well in their own special environments. Grape stems are long and viney. Grape stems have tendrils that allow the plants to hold on to other structures in their environment and grow up toward the sunshine. Hawthorn stems have large thorns that help protect them from being damaged by animals in their environment.

At the end of stems are buds. **Terminal buds** are the ones that let a plant stem grow taller. They are found at the tip of the stem or twig. **Lateral buds** form back along the stem, away from the terminal bud. These lateral buds will grow to form branches, leaves, and flowers. Lateral buds are attached to the stems at **nodes**. The areas in between the nodes are called the **internodal sections** of the stems. Buds may be covered with **bud scales** to protect them and allow them to grow undamaged.

Remember that stems are one of the three parts of plants that are called the vegetative matter.

Here's an interesting fact or two:

In the 1880s, European farmers grew only a few types of potatoes.
In 1845, most of the potato crop was destroyed by a disease.
Many people starved because they had no other food.
Farmers in Peru grow more than 3,000 different kinds of potatoes.
If one type is affected by a disease, they can eat another kind.

Name _____ Date _____

For the student:

1. What are the three jobs of a stem?

_____

_____

_____

2. What is xylem tissue?

_____

_____

3. What is phloem tissue?

_____

_____

4. What is cambium?

_____

_____

5. What is the difference between an herbaceous stem and a woody stem?

_____

_____

6. What is an aerial stem? Can you name an example?

_____

_____

7. What is a runner?

_____

_____

8. What is a rhizome?

_____

_____

9. What is an example of a tuber?

_____

_____

10. How have grape stems adapted to get more sunlight?

_____

_____

Activities:

Observing the functions of stems using celery

1. Split a stalk of celery for about four to five inches from the bottom. Do not cut it all the way to the top. Put one side of the stalk into a container with red-dyed water. Put the other side into a container with blue-dyed water. Observe the celery after 24 hours. Record your results.

2. Cut a notch or several notches in the side of a stalk of celery. Put the celery in colored water. Observe the celery after 24 hours. Record your results.

3. Place the leafy end of the celery in the colored water. Observe the celery after 24 hours. Record your results.

Here's an interesting fact or two:

When one oak tree is cut down, it may affect as many as 280 other species. All of the species are connected to the tree in some way in a food web.

Pieces of the Puzzle: Parts of a Plant, The Fast Food Industry: "Leaf" It to Me

You have already learned about the roots and stems of plants. Along with the leaves, they make up the vegetative matter in a plant. Now, let's take a closer look at plant leaves.

Leaves have one very important job to do: they make the food that the plant needs to stay alive! Food is made in a process called photosynthesis, which will be discussed later in this book.

Parts of a Leaf

Most leaves have two important parts: the **blade** and the **petiole**. The blade is the flat, thin, green part of the leaf. The petiole is the stalk or stem that attaches the blade to the stem of the plant. Some leaves have another part called a **stipule**. This looks like a tiny leaf that is attached at the point where the petiole joins the plant stem. If you look carefully at a rose, you will probably see a stipule very easily!

Leaf Structures

Let's try to take a closer look at the structures in the blade of a leaf. Let's imagine a cross-section of a leaf blade under a microscope. If we start at the top, we may find a layer of wax-like stuff that is usually called **cuticle**. The waxy cuticle helps prevent too much water from evaporating from the leaf. You should notice that this layer is transparent, so sunlight can get right through it.

Just below the cuticle, we find our first layer of plant cells. This is called the **upper epidermis**, and this is where the **cutin** is made, which makes up the cuticle we just talked about. This epidermis is also transparent, allowing in the sunlight.

We come next to the middle layers of the leaf blade. This area is called the **mesophyll**. It has a layer of **palisade cells** near the upper epidermis and **spongy cells** below them. These two kinds of tissue contain a green chemical called **chlorophyll**. Chlorophyll is needed to trap the sun's energy so a plant can make its food. Only plants with chlorophyll are able to produce their own food. This area, called the mesophyll, has lots of spaces for air, as well as vascular bundles of xylem and phloem. These bundles make up the veins that you may have noticed in leaves. Remember that xylem tissue is responsible for bringing water from the roots of the plant to the leaves, and that phloem tissue is responsible for taking the food from the leaves to the other parts of the plant.

Finally, below the mesophyll, there is a final layer called the **lower epidermis**. This layer has tiny holes in it called **stomata**. A leaf may have between 9,000 and 70,000 stomata per square centimeter, so they must be really tiny! On either side of the stomata, there are two **guard cells**. They determine the size of the stomata. When the guard cells are full of water, they swell up and the stomata open wide. When the guard cells are drier, they are smaller and the stomata close up. Normally, the size of the stomata is determined by the amount of daylight, darkness, and the temperature of the environment.

Why do plants need holes in the bottoms of their leaves? Plants need **carbon dioxide** to make their food. They get that carbon dioxide from the environment. The carbon dioxide comes in through the stomata. Plants make extra oxygen when they make their food. They give some of that oxygen back to the environment. The oxygen exits the leaves through the stomata, as well. Finally, the plant roots bring lots of water into the plant. Some of that water is not needed. It evaporates back into the atmosphere through the stomata. This evaporation of water is known as **transpiration**.

You might be interested to know just how much some plants transpire. Scientists believe that one apple tree will transpire as much as 200 liters of water during its growing season.

Shapes of Leaves

Leaves have the same basic parts, but they are not all put together in the same way. Some leaves have only one leaf blade. These are called **simple leaves**. An elm leaf is a good example of a simple leaf blade.

Some leaves have more than one blade attached to a single petiole. These are called **compound leaves**. If the leaf blades are arranged in rows on opposite sides of the main vein or midrib, it is called a **pinnately compound leaf**. Take a look at a black locust or mimosa leaf. If the leaf blades start at a central point and then radiate out like a fan, it is called a **palmately compound leaf**. Take a look at a horse chestnut or hickory leaf.

Leaf Veins

We know that scientists are very observant people. We also know that scientists love to classify things. So, not only do they identify the parts of the leaves and classify the arrangement of leaf blades, scientists also classify the arrangement of veins in a leaf. Remember that the veins are really bundles of xylem and phloem needed to transport food and water throughout the leaf. These veins have two more important jobs to do, as well. They support the leaf and hold it up so that as much surface as possible can be exposed to the sun. That's very important in making food to stay alive!

First, let's consider the veins on a leaf from a corn plant. The veins are side-by-side or parallel to each other. The veins run from the base of the leaf to the tip of the leaf. These veins, appropriately enough, are called **parallel veins**.

If we take a look at the veins in an elm leaf, we should see a single main vein with smaller veins branching off of it. This is called a **net-veined leaf** because the veins form a network. There are two types of net-veined leaves. An elm leaf has just one main vein with smaller veins branching or radiating off of it. This is a **pinnately-veined leaf**. If we take a look at a maple leaf, we will notice several main veins with smaller veins branching off of them. Again, this is a net-veined leaf. This time, however, because there is more than one main vein, this is known as a **palmately-veined leaf**.

Leaf Arrangements

Leaves may be attached to the stem of their plants in different ways. Some leaves are attached in an alternating or spiral pattern. If the first leaf is attached to one side of the stem and the next leaf is attached on the other side, these are called **alternating leaves**. If the leaves seem to circle around the plant at their points of attachment, they are known as **spiralling leaves**. If two leaves attach at the same level, but on opposite sides of the stem, they are called **oppositional leaves**. If the next pair of oppositional leaves attaches at a right angle to a previous pair, they are called **decussate leaves**. If more than two leaves attach to the stem at the same level, they are called **whorled leaves**. Take a close look at the plants in your classroom, school yard, or lawn at home. Can you find examples of alternating, spiraling, oppositional, decussate, and whorled leaves?

Leaf Adaptations

Plants can be found in many different kinds of environments. Some plant leaves have special adaptations that allow the plant to survive better in extreme weather conditions. Leaves with large, flat blades can absorb lots of sunlight. They are more likely to have problems with water evaporation, so they might not do well in dry areas. Cacti have adapted to their environment by becoming almost leafless plants.

Cold winter winds are very dry. They steal moisture from plants as they blow through an area. Most conifers have specially adapted leaves that look like needles. Less surface area is exposed to the wind, so there is less loss of moisture during the cold winter months.

Aloe vera plants live in very arid areas. They need to absorb as much water as possible, and they need to hold on to it for as long as possible. Aloe vera leaves are very spongy, which lets them be successful at both jobs: absorbing and holding water.

In the tropics, too much moisture can be a problem. Plants in tropical areas may have leaves that encourage water to run off the tips of the leaves. The surface of the leaf is free to absorb more sunshine, and the roots are able to absorb all the water that the plant needs.

What kinds of adaptations are needed in your area? Do you have very hot or very cold temperatures? Do you have lots of wind or lots of rain? Do you have a dry climate or lots of snow? Take a look at the plants around you and see what kinds of special adaptations they have to better survive the conditions of their environment.

Here's an interesting fact or two:

The largest plant leaves are found on the raffia palm plants.
The leaves may be 65 feet long.
They may be eight feet wide.

Name _____ Date _____

For the student:

Complete each of the following sentences.

1. The most important job of a leaf is to _____.

2. The two basic parts of a leaf are the _____ and _____.

3. The waxy cuticle on the top of a leaf helps prevent _____

_____.

4. Chlorophyll can be found in _____ and _____ cells.

5. The lower epidermis has tiny holes that are called _____ .

6. The size of stomata is determined by _____ , _____ ,

and _____ .

7. Stomata get _____ _____ from the environment and give

_____ to the environment.

8. Evaporation of water from a plant is called _____ .

9. Simple leaves have _____ leaf blade.

10. Compound leaves have more than one leaf blade attached to a single _____ .

11. Leaf veins that are side-by-side are called _____ veins.

12. A leaf with branching veins that form a network is called a _____ leaf.

13. A leaf with one main vein and several smaller veins branching off of it is called a

_____ veined leaf.

14. A leaf with several main veins and smaller veins branching off of them is called a

_____ veined leaf.

15. Alternating leaves are attached to one side of the stem and then the _____ .

16. Oppositional leaves attach on opposite sides of the stem at the same _____ .

17. Conifer leaves are adapted for areas with cold _____ _____ .

18. Cactus plants are almost leafless to adapt to areas with little _____ .

19. Tropical plants may be adapted to let _____ run off the tips of the leaves.

20. Aloe vera plants have spongy leaves to _____ and _____ water.

Name _____ Date _____

Activities:

Observing the functions of leaves

1. Do plants lose water?
      Obtain two similar plants.
      Place a plastic bag over the top of one plant.
      Attach the bag around the base of the stem.
      Observe both plants and the bag.
      Set both plants in the sun.
      After 24 hours, observe both plants and the bag again.
      Record your observations.
          A. What was the substance in the bag? _____

_____

          B. How did the water get into the bag? _____

_____

2. Can plants live without leaves?
      Obtain two similar plants.
      Remove all the leaves from one plant at the point where the petiole attaches to the stem.
      Place both plants in a sunny location.
      Keep both plants watered.
      Observe the plants for one week.
      Record your observations.
          A. Did both plants thrive? _____

_____

          B. Why did the plant die? _____

_____

3. Do plants need air to live?
      Obtain two similar plants. (Mung bean plants will work well, however, they should be at least two weeks old.)
      Spread petroleum jelly on the bottom side of the leaves of one plant (B).
      Spread petroleum jelly on the top side of the leaves of the other plant (A).
      Mark each plant with a stake to keep them properly identified.
      Place the plants in a sunny location and keep them watered.

Name_____ Date _____

Observe the plants for one week.
Record your observations.

A. Did both plants thrive? _____

_____

B. Why did one plant thrive? _____

_____

4. Do plants give off oxygen?

Obtain one plant.

Water the plant and place it in a holding tray.

Place a beaker with four ounces of lime water in the holding tray.
(Bromothymol blue solution may be used instead.)

Place a ruler or wooden rod vertically in the holding tray.

Place a plastic bag over the plant, ruler, and lime water. (The ruler will prevent the plant from collapsing under the weight of the bag.)

Tape the bag all around the edges of the holding tray so that no air can get in or out.

Place the experiment in a dark closet.

Observe the experiment after 48 hours.

Record your observations.

A. What happened to the lime water? _____

_____

B. What gas has the plant released into the air in the bag? _____

_____

Parts of a Leaf

Cross-section of a Leaf

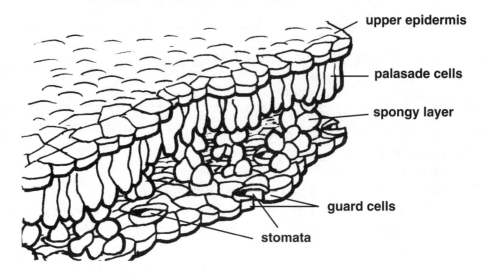

upper epidermis

palasade cells

spongy layer

guard cells

stomata

Kinds of Leaves

Simple Leaves

Compound Leaves

Pinnated Leaves

Palmated Leaves

Veins in Leaves

Parallel Veins

Net-veined Leaves

Pinnated Veins

Palmated Veins

Leaf Attachments

Alternating Leaves

Spiraling Leaves

Oppositional Leaves

Decussate Leaves

Whorled Leaves

Pieces of the Puzzle: Parts of a Plant,
A Rose by Any Other Name: Flowers

Now that you know about roots, stems, and leaves, it is time to study flowers. Do you already know the names of some flowers? Are there flowers growing in your yard or in your home? Maybe you have even gotten flowers for a special day or event. Do you know why plants have flowers? Do you know what all the special parts of a flower are?

Let's think back for a moment to our definition of an organism. We decided that all organisms must be able to reproduce. They must be able to make more organisms just like themselves! Plants are organisms, so plants must have some way to reproduce. Some kinds of plants make flowers. Those flowers have the special job of reproduction. Those flowers make sure that the flowering plants can make more flowering plants just like themselves!

Many flowers have four parts to them: the calyx, the corolla, the stamens, and the pistil. Let's take a closer look at each one of those parts.

The Calyx

The **calyx** is green and looks like leaves. Sometimes the calyx is called the sepals. The calyx has two jobs. The first job of the calyx is to protect the flower bud until it is the right time for the bud to open. The calyx is wrapped around the flower bud before it opens. After the bud opens and blooms, it needs something to hold it up, so the second job of the calyx is to spread open at the base of the flower and hold up the flower on the plant.

The Corolla

The **corolla** consists of all the petals of a flower. Many flowers have bright, colorful petals, while some flowers are dull and we hardly even notice them. Did you know that grasses have flowers? They are not very bright or very colorful!

Have you ever gotten a letter in the mail? It probably came in an envelope. The envelope protected the paper inside. Scientists call the calyx and the corolla the **floral envelope** of a plant. Remember the calyx protects the beautiful flower bud inside!

The Stamens

The **stamens** are the male reproductive parts of a flower. Each stamen actually consists of two parts put together. The **anther** is an enlarged part of the stamen. It grows on a thin, stalk-like part that is called the **filament**. The anther produces **pollen**. Pollen contains **sperm cells**. The sperm cells are very important in the reproduction of a flowering plant.

30

The Pistil

The female part of a flower is called the **pistil**. A pistil has three important parts. At the top of the pistil is a flattened part that is called the **stigma**. The stigma is attached to a tube, which is called the **style**. At the base of the style is the **ovary**. The ovary contains the **egg cells** of the flower. This is where the final stages of reproduction occur.

Some plants do not have all the flower parts on one plant. These plants make **incomplete flowers**. For example, corn makes incomplete flowers in two different places on each corn plant. The male flowers are in the tassel at the top of the stalk. The female flowers are in the ears farther down along the stalk. Many trees also have incomplete flowers. One tree may make the male flower while another tree makes the female flower. Both trees must be present for the flowers to bloom and for the tree to reproduce.

Using the information you have learned in this lesson, try to label the parts of the flower in the illustration below.

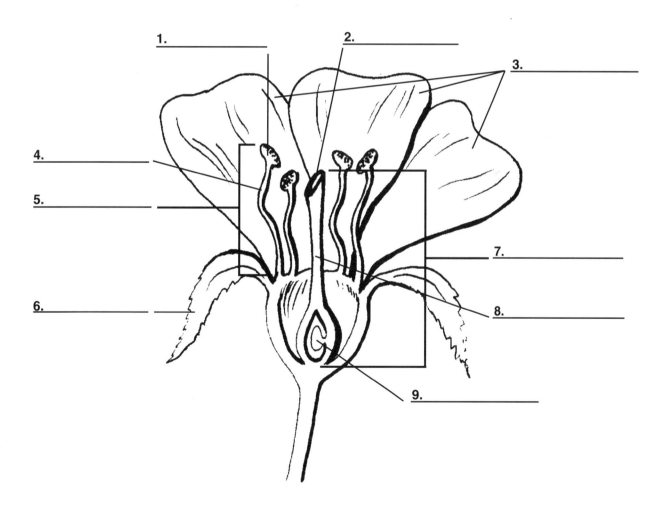

Name_____ Date _____

For the Student:

Match each description with the correct flower part.

_____ 1. Green, leaf-like structure that provides
protection and support for the flower
bud

A. Anther

B. Calyx

_____ 2. All of the petals of a flower

C. Corolla

_____ 3. The male organs in a flower

D. Flower

_____ 4. The female organs in a flower

E. Ovary

_____ 5. The part of a flower that produces
pollen

F. Pistil

G. Pollen

_____ 6. The part of a flower that contains sperm
cells

H. Stamens

_____ 7. The top part of the female organ

I. Stigma

_____ 8. The tube in the female organ

J. Style

_____ 9. The base of the female organ

_____ 10. The reproductive part of many plants

Activities:

Observing, Listing, and Understanding Flowers

1. Have the students list as many flowers as possible. Divide the class into teams. Have each team develop a list. Distribute petal-shaped pieces of paper to each team. (Copies of the petals below can be made on colored paper, or have students use crayons or colored pencils to color copies of the petals.) Have the students write the name of a different flower on each petal. See which team can make a flower with the greatest number of petals by listing the greatest variety of flowers.

2. Have students name their favorite flowers. Have the students write a short narrative describing the flower and why they chose that particular flower as their favorite.

3. Develop lists of flowers by color. Develop a rainbow bulletin board. Using pictures of flowers from magazines and garden catalogs, group the pictures according to the colors of the rainbow (red, orange, yellow, green, blue, indigo, and violet).

4. Contact a local florist. Have the florist speak to the class, explaining the type of work done and the kind of training required. Ask the florist if you may have any old flowers to examine the flower parts.

5. Contact a local nursery. Ask the nursery person to discuss plants that produce incomplete flowers and how that must be taken into account when planning a landscape.

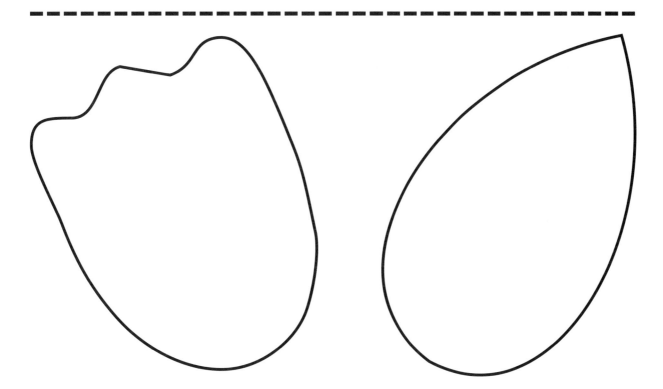

Pieces of the Puzzle: Parts of a Plant, Starting Over: Seeds

It's 4:00 in the afternoon and you are hungry. You head for the fridge for a snack, and you see a juicy red apple. You quickly wash off the apple and then sink your teeth into it. It is delicious, and the juice from the apple runs down your chin. You eat around the whole thing until there is nothing left but the core. You notice the tiny blackish-brown seeds, and it makes you wonder, "Why do plants have seeds?".

Why Seeds?

Seeds contain the young plant that allows the organism to reproduce. If you were to plant the apple seeds in the right kind of soil, with the right temperature and the right amount of water, you might find yourself growing a whole new apple tree!

We put seeds to good use, too, but not always to grow new plants. People and other animals use some kinds of seeds for food. Have you ever eaten a walnut? You were actually eating the seed of the walnut tree. Have you ever eaten flour? Wheat seeds are ground into flour and are used to make many kinds of food.

Seeds come in a variety of sizes and shapes. Have you ever eaten a strawberry? Think of the tiny seeds along the outside of the fruit. Have you ever had an avocado? The middle of that fruit has a much larger brown seed. Did you know that the size of the seed really has nothing to do with the size of the adult plant when it finishes growing? Redwood trees are the tallest plants in the world, and yet, they start growing from tiny seeds that are only one-sixteenth of an inch long. Those trees sure have to live a long time to get to their full height!

Kinds of Seeds

Scientists have found two basic kinds of seeds. The first kind is called a **naked seed**. Cone-bearing plants have naked seeds. Their seeds develop inside the cones. They form along the upper side of the cone's scales.

The second kind of seed is called an **enclosed seed**. Flowering plants have enclosed seeds. They are surrounded by an ovary. Some of the ovaries form **fleshy fruits**. You may have seen many of them. They include apples, most berries, and grapes. Other ovaries form **dry fruits**. Have you ever seen bean or pea pods after they have been picked and have sat around for a day or two? They are dry and show the shape of the seeds inside them! The final kind of ovary is called an **aggregate fruit**. Instead of having just one ovary with one or more seeds, aggregate fruits have separate ovaries bundled together. Each ovary has its own seed. Raspberries are aggregate fruits. Maybe that is why it is so easy to get raspberry seeds stuck in our teeth.

Parts of Seeds

Seeds have three parts. The first part is the **seed coat**. I never like to go out in cold and snowy weather without my coat. It protects me and keeps me warm. A seed coat also protects the tender, tiny parts inside it. The seed coat gives those tiny parts a chance to survive until the conditions are just right for the seed to grow into a new plant.

Inside the seed coat is the second part, the **embryo**. This contains all the parts that are needed to become a new plant. One part is called the **radicle**. This will become the roots for the new plant. Another part is called the **hypocotyl**, which will become the lower stem. The upper stem and the leaves will form from the third part, which is called the **epicotyl**. Attached to the embryo inside the seed coat are the **cotyledon**. These are the tiny seed leaves that absorb food and allow the plant to begin its growth.

In many seeds there is also special tissue for storing food. Flowering plants have food storage tissue that is called **endosperm**. Cone-bearing plants also have some food storage tissue, and it is known as **megagametophyte**.

Can you label the parts of a seed shown in the illustration below?

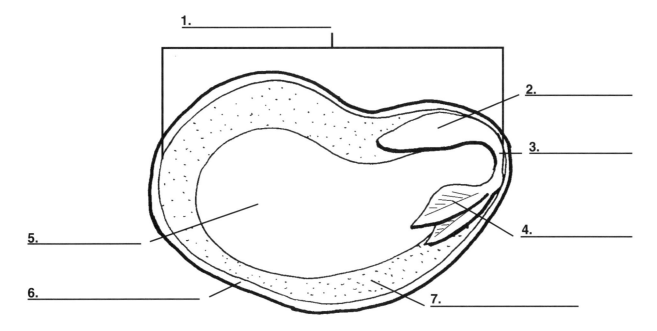

1. _____

2. _____

3. _____

4. _____

5. _____

6. _____

7. _____

Here's an interesting fact or two:

Tobacco seeds are among the tiniest seeds.
Two thousand five hundred seeds can fit in one pod.
Each pod is only three-fourths of an inch long!
Coconut seeds are among the heaviest.
A coconut can weigh up to 20 pounds!

Name _____ Date _____

For the Student:

1. Why are seeds important to a plant?

_____

_____

2. What are three kinds of seeds that you eat?

_____

_____

3. Do tiny seeds always grow into tiny plants? How do you know?

_____

_____

_____

4. I have a hemlock tree in my front yard. Does it have naked seeds or enclosed seeds? How do you know?

_____

_____

_____

5. What are three kinds of ovaries that surround enclosed seeds?

_____

_____

_____

6. Which part of a seed protects the seed?

_____

7. What do the radicle, the hypocotyl, and the epicotyl form?

_____

8. What does the endosperm do in flowering plants?

_____

_____

Gone With the Wind: Seed Dispersal

If all plant seeds just fell to the ground around the parent plant, we would have a real problem. The new plants would all try to grow in the same area. There would not be enough water, minerals, or sunlight for all of them to survive. They would be competing with each other, and some of them would lose. The losers would die. How, then, can plants survive? How can they grow in areas away from their parent plants? The answer is **seed dispersal**. The word *dispersal* means "carrying away." The seeds are carried away from the area where the parent plant is growing. How can the seeds be carried away?

Wind

One way the seeds can move is by using the wind. Maple, ash, and elm tree seeds all have special wings. When the wind blows, the seeds are carried off the trees and are blown away. They may land on the ground quite a distance from the adult tree. They will have more room, water, minerals, and sunshine, so they will have a better chance of surviving. In a similar way, cotton, milkweed, and dandelion seeds have long, silky hairs that are easily blown by the wind. Some of them act like parachutes, carrying the seeds over long distances.

Water

Seeds can also move on water. Coconuts are heavy seeds, but they float! When they fall off the tree, they may land in the water and be carried a long way by the currents.

Touch

Some plants are sensitive to touch. If a Touch-me-not is only slightly bumped, it will shoot its seeds out away from the parent plant. This is self-dispersal!

Animals

Animals are important for good seed dispersal. Animals eat many fruits that have seeds inside them. Sometimes the seed coats will protect the seeds as they go through the animal's digestive system. They exit the animal's body with the waste material. These seeds may have been carried a long way from "home." If conditions are right, the seeds may begin to grown in their new "home." Some seeds have bristles, hooks, or barbs on them. Have you ever been for a walk in the Autumn and come home with cockleburs or grass seeds stuck on your pants or in your shoe laces? If so, you were an agent in seed dispersal. Other animals wandering through the woods will disperse the seeds in a similar way. Finally, think about squirrels. They find nuts and other types of seeds and hide them away for future meals. Sometimes they forget about the nuts, and those seeds are able to grow into new plants.

Name _____ Date _____

For the Student:

1. What are three things that plants need to grow well?

_____

_____

2. What happens if too many plants are trying to grow in the same area?

_____

_____

_____

3. What does *dispersal* mean?

_____

_____

4. List three ways that nature can disperse seeds.

_____

_____

_____

5. How can people disperse seeds?

_____

_____

_____

6. Why is seed dispersal beneficial to plants?

_____

_____

_____

Activities:

Collecting, Comparing, Identifying, and Observing Seeds

1. Get a collection of seeds in packets. Remove the seeds from the packets. Be sure to develop an answer key. Set out the seed packets and the seeds. Have students try to match the seeds to the adult plants pictured on the packets.

2. Compare wet and dry been seeds. Soak several bean seeds in warm water overnight. Leave an equal number of bean seeds dry. Compare the seed coats of the dry and wet beans. Open some of the wet bean seeds. Try to identify the parts of the seed. Add a couple of drops of iodine to the seed. If it turns blue, it indicates the presence of starch. Why would a bean seed need starch?

3. Prepare some potting soil in a large pot. Plant about 20 bean seeds in the soil. Water the soil and keep it in a warm, sunny location. Every other day, remove two seeds from the soil. Observe any changes in the seeds. Record your observations. (A Polaroid camera is a nice tool for recording the changes in the seed development.)

4. Take a walk in a weedy field. Prepare the students, asking them to wear long pants and old socks and shoes for your field trip. Upon returning to the classroom, collect any seeds caught on pants, socks, or shoes. Be sure to check shirt or sweater sleeves, too. Sort the seeds, counting the number of kinds of seeds. Try to identify the source of the seeds.

All Organisms Reproduce: Sexual Reproduction

Remember we learned all organisms have six features in common. We learned one of those features was the ability to reproduce. We also learned plants are organisms, so plants must reproduce. Plants create more plants in one of two ways: sexual reproduction and asexual reproduction. First, let's learn about sexual reproduction.

Sexual reproduction involves the joining of two cells. A male cell and a female cell will join, making a new organism in a process called fertilization. Flowering plants, cone-bearing plants, ferns, and mosses are all capable of sexual reproduction.

Flowering plants

Remember the stamens are the male reproductive parts of a flower. The stamens actually consist of two parts: the filament and the anther. The anther produces pollen, which contains the sperm cells. The sperm cells are the male cells needed for sexual reproduction.

Also remember the pistil is the female reproductive part of a flower. The pistil actually consists of three parts: the stigma, the style, and the ovary. The ovary contains the egg cells. The egg cells are the female cells needed for sexual reproduction.

In order for a flowering plant to reproduce, the pollen from the stamens must travel to the pistil. When the pollen arrives at the pistil, it will stick to the stigma at the top of the pistil. This process is called **pollination**.

Flowers may need help to get the pollen from the stamens to the pistil. Luckily, they have lots of help close by. Wind is often a good pollinator. The pollen grains of many plants are often tiny and light. The wind can easily carry them from the stamens to the pistil. Insects are often good pollinators, as well. When insects travel to a flower searching for food, some of the pollen from that flower may stick to their bodies or legs. When they travel to the next flower, pollen from the first flower may stick to the stigma of the second flower. Pollination is complete! Finally, some birds are pollinators. Like insects, they search out food in many flowers. When they travel from blossom to blossom, they carry pollen grains in their feathers and on their legs. Insects and birds are responsible for pollinating flowers over greater distances than wind. They may fly a long way from one flower to the next. The wind will usually only carry pollen grains for a short distance.

Some flowers are **self-pollinators**. They have everything they need in just one plant. The male and female cells are right there, and the pollen grains will travel from the stamens of the plant to the pistil of the same plant. Other flowers are **cross-pollinators**. They need another plant to make the pollination complete. Cross-pollinators often have large, colorful blooms. They also may have a sweet scent and sweeter nectar. They need to attract insects and birds to their flowers so these animals can pick up the pollen grains and carry them to another flower.

Once the pollen grains have arrived at the stigma, a pollen tube begins to form. The pollen tube travels down the style to the ovary. In the ovary, each pollen tube will try to find an egg cell. The sperm cell will travel down the pollen tube into the egg. This process is called **fertilization**. When the egg cell is fertilized by the sperm cell, a new plant begins to form as a seed. Reproduction has been completed.

Cone-Bearing Plants

You have probably seen many kinds of cones. Some of them are long and thin, and others are small and round. Did you know that each kind of cone-bearing plant actually makes two kinds of cones? These plants make male and female cones. The male cones are usually smaller and softer. The female cones are larger and harder. The female cones are the ones that we know the best.

Wind is very helpful in pollinating cone-bearing plants. When the pollen grains are ripe in the male cone, the wind will carry them from the male cone to the female cone. When the pollen lands on the female cone, pollination has occurred. The pollen grain will form a pollen tube. When the pollen tube finds the female's egg cell, fertilization takes place, and a new seed begins to form.

Ferns and Mosses

Ferns and mosses go through cycles that make two different plants. Both of these plants are needed for sexual reproduction to occur. On one plant, spores form on the undersides of the plant's leaves. The spores ripen and fall to the ground. When the conditions are right in the ground, a new plant begins to grow from a spore. This plant is called a **gametophyte**. The gametophyte plant makes both male and female cells. When there is enough moisture, the male and female cells unite, and fertilization takes place. A new plant is formed.

Name _____ Date _____

For the Student:

1. What are the two ways that plants can reproduce?

_____

_____

2. What are four kinds of plants that are capable of sexual reproduction?

_____

_____

3. What are the male and female reproductive parts of a flower?

_____

_____

4. What is pollination?

_____

_____

5. What are three "helpers" for plant pollination?

_____

_____

6. In tropical rain forests, there is not much wind. Why is it important to plants that the tropical rain forests have lots of insects and birds?

_____

_____

7. Why do some plants have large, sweet-smelling flowers with sweet nectar?

_____

_____

8. What is fertilization?

_____

_____

9. Why do cone-bearing plants have two different kinds of cones?

_____

_____

10. Which kinds of plants go through a cycle, making two different kinds of plants for fertilization?

_____

_____

All Organisms Reproduce: Asexual Reproduction

You have just learned how plants can reproduce using male and female cells. This is called sexual reproduction. Now, let's see what we can learn about **asexual reproduction**.

Budding

On a recent walk through a sand prairie, I learned why it is important to wear good shoes and socks. Scattered along the ground were many prickly pear cactus plants. They had long thorns sticking out, which made it hard to walk through them. My shoes were good protection, but my poor ankles were sore by the time I got home because they were not properly protected by socks.

I was curious about the cacti growing in the sand, so I stopped to take a closer look. I realized that the cacti were made of pads. Small, new pads seemed to be growing out the sides and along the top of the older, larger pads. I learned later that those smaller pads were **buds**. The buds could fall off the main plant and take root in the sand, forming a new cactus plant. I had been studying one kind of asexual reproduction: budding.

"Eyes"

Potatoes use another kind of bud, which we call eyes. Have you ever noticed an old potato? You have probably seen funny-looking white spots growing out of its sides. The white spots look like they are growing out of dimples. Those dimples are actually called the **eyes**. The funny white spots are new roots. Here's an idea. Cut up your old potato into several pieces, leaving a chunk of potato with each eye. Plant the potatoes in some dirt or in the ground. If you can be patient and wait a while, you should notice some plants poking up through the dirt. Those are new potato plants. Once again, this is an example of asexual reproduction.

Runners

Last spring, I planted strawberries in my garden patch. I put in 25 plants because I thought that would give me enough strawberries to eat. This year, when I went to clean up the strawberry patch, I noticed there were more than 25 plants! I went back to the nursery where I had gotten the plants, and I asked the garden center manager about the extra plants. He explained to me that strawberries can reproduce using **runners**. Runners are stems that grow along the ground instead of growing up from the ground. When the runners touch the ground, they can start growing new roots. When the roots are well-established, a new strawberry plant will grow. The runner will eventually die off, and the new plant will be separated from its parent plant. This is another kind of asexual reproduction.

The garden center manager told me about some other plants that can grow from runners. He told me that some kinds of grasses spread with runners. He said some ferns, irises, and blueberry plants use runners to reproduce, as well.

43

Natural Layering

I have some beautiful yellow forsythia bushes in my yard. In the early spring, they shine in the sunlight. They brighten up my day. The branches of the forsythia bushes grow up and then drape down toward the ground, which makes them look very graceful. It also helps the forsythia bush reproduce. If the tips of the branches can reach the ground, they can form roots. The roots will develop, and a new forsythia bush will form at that spot. This is called **natural layering**.

Raspberry bushes will do the same thing. If you want to expand your raspberry patch, you can bend the branches down and anchor them near the ground. When the tips of the branches reach the ground, they will start to make new plants.

Bulbs

Some plants grow from **bulbs**. Tulips are a good example. If you plant the bulbs in the ground in the fall, you should have beautiful tulips in your garden the next spring. (The bulbs have to go through a cold treatment, so this will only work in colder climates!) The bulbs contain the food for the new plant to use until it grows big enough leaves to make its own food. After a while, the bulb itself will grow. A new, smaller bulb will form along the side of the first bulb. In future years, two or more stems may grow from the spot where you first planted the bulb. If you dig it up, you can break apart the new bulbs from the old one, and you will have two or more bulbs for the price of one. This is another example of asexual reproduction.

Activities:

1. Purchase some carrots with the tops still attached. Cut off the top of each carrot, leaving about one inch of vegetable attached to the leaves. Suspend the carrot top in water, using toothpicks to hold it in place. Observe and record what happens.

2. Grow several bean plants from seed. When the plants are four to five inches tall, cut the stems of the plants. Place the cut stems of three or four plants in moist soil. Place the cut stems of three or four other plants in water. Observe and record what happens.

3. Remove leaves from a jade, ivy, or philodendron plant. Place the leaves in moist soil or growing medium. Observe and record what happens.

4. Contact a local nursery. Arrange for a field trip to observe cuttings being taken or rooted.

5. Ask a local nurseryperson to speak to the class about plant propogation.

6. Research hydroponics.

7. Research tissue culture as a new form of plant propogation.

Name _____ Date _____

For the Student:

1. What is an example of a plant that can reproduce by budding?

_____

_____

2. How can I get new potato plants from an old potato?

_____

_____

3. What is a runner?

_____

_____

4. What are two kinds of plants that reproduce using runners?

_____

_____

5. How can I grow new raspberry bushes from my old bushes?

_____

_____

6. Tulips grow from bulbs. What are some other flowers that grow from bulbs?

_____

_____

Match the definitions in Column B with the correct terms in Column A.

Column A	Column B
_____ 7. Asexual	A. Part of a tulip that contains the food for the new plant
_____ 8. Budding	B. Stems that grow along the ground and produce new roots
_____ 9. Bulb	C. When the tips of branches drape over to reach the ground and start to form roots
_____ 10. Eyes	D. Reproduction that does not involve male and female cells combining
_____ 11. Natural Layering	E. Dimples on a potato from which new roots will grow
_____ 12. Runners	F. When new, smaller pads or segments develop on a plant, fall off, and take root

Mary, Mary...How Does Your Garden Grow? Germination of Plants

Now that you know what a plant is and are familiar with the parts of a plant, it is time to learn how a plant grows. To understand how a plant grows, you must learn about germination.

Germination is the early growth of a plant from a seed. Germination depends on three factors: having the right temperature, the right amount of moisture, and enough oxygen. Let's take a closer look at these three factors.

The first factor is **temperature**. Most seeds need a temperature between 65 and 85 degrees Fahrenheit for germination to take place. Plants that grow in colder climates often germinate at colder temperatures. They may go through a period of inactivity before they germinate. The seeds may form on a plant in the fall and be inactive through the winter. As the soil and air temperatures warm up in the spring, the seeds may germinate, and the new plants begin to grow. Plants that grow in warm areas, such as the tropical rain forests, will germinate at warmer temperatures. They may not experience a period of inactivity.

The second important factor is **moisture**. The seed gets its moisture from the ground. It absorbs the moisture, and it swells. The moisture softens the seed coat, and the swelling causes the seed coat to burst open. The young plant, or **embryo**, is able to move out of the seed coat and begin to grow. If a seed has too much moisture, it may rot before it has a chance to begin growing. If a seed does not have enough moisture, it may germinate very slowly, or it may not germinate at all.

Finally, **oxygen** is important for germination. The seed must go through many changes as it grows and becomes a new plant. Oxygen is a necessary part of many of those changes. Without oxygen, the changes cannot take place, and the seed cannot germinate. It cannot become a new plant.

When the three conditions are right, the seed opens, and the embryo emerges. The **hypocotyl** comes out of the seed. This will become the main root. Its job is to anchor the seed and provide the water and minerals that the embryo needs to grow. Next, the **epicotyl** emerges. This grows up and becomes the upper part of the plant. It contains the first leaves.

Let's think for a moment about farmers. They must know a lot about the germination of seeds. They must know a lot about the seeds they want to plant. They must know about the temperature of the air and soil. They must know a lot about the amount of moisture in the soil. They want everything to be right before they start to plant their crops. If a farmer puts his crops in too early in the spring, the soil may be too cold for good germination. If there is too much rain after a crop is planted, the seeds may rot before they can germinate. If there is not enough rain after a crop is planted, the seeds may not have enough moisture to germinate on time. The farmer needs to know a lot about the weather, the soil, and the kinds of seeds he is planting. His livelihood depends on it.

Name _____ Date _____

For the Student:

1. What is germination?

_____

_____

2. What are the three factors needed for germination of a seed?

_____

_____

3. Why might seeds in northern Minnesota germinate at lower temperatures than seeds in southern Texas?

_____

_____

4. Where do seeds get the moisture they need for germination?

_____

_____

5. What happens if a seed does not get enough moisture?

_____

_____

6. What happens if a seed has too much moisture?

_____

_____

7. Why do seeds need oxygen?

_____

_____

8. What is the hypocotyl?

_____

_____

9. What is the epicotyl?

_____

_____

10. List some of the things farmers must know and pay attention to.

_____

_____

_____

Activities:

Do all seeds germinate at the same rate?

Get a variety of seeds. Fill styrofoam cups half full of potting soil. Label each cup with the type of seed that will be planted in it and the date of the planting. Place three or four seeds in each styrofoam cup. Water each cup with the same amount of water. Place the cups in a warm, sunny location. Be sure to keep the soil in the cups moist, but use the same amount of water when watering each cup. Observe the cups each day. Record the emergence of the seeds. Compare the length of time for the seeds to germinate.

Do seeds really need moisture to germinate?

Get two dozen bean seeds and six glass jars. Place a paper towel around the inside of each jar. Place four seeds between the paper towel and the sides of each jar. Moisten the paper towel in three jars and leave the paper towel dry in the other three jars. Place the jars in a warm, sunny location. Observe the seeds to see which ones will germinate.

Do seeds really need warm temperatures to germinate?

Get two dozen bean seeds and six glass jars. Prepare the jars and seeds as you did in the previous activity. Moisten the towels in all six jars. Place three of the jars in a warm, sunny location. Place the other three jars in a refrigerator. Keep the paper towels equally moist in all jars. Observe the jars to see which seeds will germinate.

The Great Chefs of the Plant World: Photosynthesis and Respiration

When a seed germinates, a new plant emerges from the ground. At first, the new plant uses the food stored in the seed. When the first leaves emerge, however, the plant begins to make its own food. The process that plants use to make their own food is called **photosynthesis**.

Photosynthesis is a process which includes a chemical change. As a result of the chemical change, food is made. In order to photosynthesize, a plant must have a special chemical called **chlorophyll**. This chemical is found in the plant's cells. It is stored inside small cell bodies called **chloroplasts**.

When I want to make a cake, I gather together certain ingredients. I measure the ingredients out and mix them together in the right amounts. Then I put the ingredients in the oven and wait until they have cooked long enough. When the ingredients are done being cooked, I have a delicious cake that gives me the energy I need to wash up the dishes!

Plants follow similar steps when they are making their own food. First, they have to have the right "ingredients." The important ingredients for photosynthesis are carbon dioxide (CO_2) and water (H_2O). Plants get the carbon dioxide they need from the air, and they get their water from the soil. Plants must also have just the right amount of each ingredient. They need six parts of carbon dioxide and six parts of water.

Plants do not put their ingredients into an oven to cook them up. Instead, plants use their chlorophyll to trap the sun's energy. The sun's energy is then used to complete the chemical reaction, joining the carbon dioxide and water. When the reaction is complete, the plant has its food and some oxygen. The food is a form of sugar ($C_6H_{12}O_6$) that is used to build and repair the plant's cells, tissues, and organs. The sugar is also used to make cellulose. **Cellulose** is an important part of a plant's cell walls. The oxygen is released into the air for animals to breathe. The chemical reaction makes one part of sugar, but it makes six parts of oxygen.

Take a look at the whole chemical equation:
$$6\ CO_2 + 6\ H_2O \longrightarrow C_6H_{12}O_6 + 6\ O_2$$

Plants must have green leaves in order to photosynthesize, so deciduous trees will not photosynthesize when they have dropped their leaves. Photosynthesis is a process that takes place during the day, as the plants need sunlight to "bake" their food. Plants will make more food during the long days of summer than they will during the shorter days of fall or winter.

When plants are ready to build and repair their cells and tissue, they must have energy to do their work. They get their energy from their food, just like animals do. Energy is released in a process called **respiration**. There are certain "ingredients" needed for this process to take place. A plant must have food and oxygen. The food that the plants use is sugar, made during the process of photosynthesis. This sugar combines with six parts of oxygen. The oxygen is made by the plant during photosynthesis and released into the air. The oxygen is reabsorbed through the leaves of the plant.

When the sugar and the oxygen combine in a chemical reaction, energy is released. Waste products are also produced. The waste products are carbon dioxide and water. Through respiration, a plant will produce six parts of carbon dioxide and six parts of water. Both the carbon dioxide and the water are released into the air. The plant can then use the carbon dioxide again for photosynthesis.

Let's take a look at this chemical equation:

$$C_6H_{12}O_6 + 6\ O_2 \text{ ---- energy ----> } 6\ CO_2 + 6\ H_2O$$

Respiration is a process that takes place during both the day and the night. Respiration decreases during the winter months and increases in the spring and summer months.

Photosynthesis and respiration are related processes. The products made during photosynthesis are used for respiration. In turn, the products made during the process of respiration are used for photosynthesis. It is a true cycle of life.

Activities:

1. Using a well-established green plant, cover a couple of leaves with black cardboard. Be sure you cover both the top and bottom sides of the leaves. Leave the cardboard on the leaves for several days, and then remove the paper. What changes do you notice in the leaves? What happens to the leaves if you leave the paper off for several days?

2. Place a small piece of wood on a section of yard. Leave the wood on the grass for two or three days. Remove the wood and note any changes in the grass. Leave the wood off the grass. Observe the area each day. Record any changes in the grass.

3. Place a plastic bag over a leaf of a well-established green plant. Leave the bag on the leaf for several days. Observe the bag. What product is released by the plant into the bag?

Name _____ Date _____

For the Student:

1. What are photosynthesis and respiration?

_____

_____

2. What are two important "ingredients" for photosynthesis and two for respiration?

_____

_____

3. From where do those important ingredients come?

_____

_____

4. What do plants use to "bake" their food?

_____

_____

5. What two products are made in the process of photosynthesis and what two are made in respiration?

_____

_____

6. For what do plants use the sugar?

_____

_____

7. What happens to the oxygen that the plants make?

_____

_____

8. Why don't deciduous plants photosynthesize during the winter?

_____

_____

9. During what season will plants photosynthesize the most?

_____

_____

10. How are photosynthesis and respiration related?

_____

_____

_____

Where, Oh, Where Does My Little Plant Grow?
Habitats of Plants

A plant's environment includes several different factors. Weather is one of those factors. Weather includes the amount of sunlight, the range of temperature, and the amount of yearly precipitation. Soil is another factor. The other plants and animals sharing the environment are still another factor. All of the factors together are known as the **natural community**.

Scientists have divided our world into several units or parts that have similar plants, animals, and climates. These units or parts are known as **biomes**. Scientists have identified several land biomes and two aquatic biomes. Let's get an idea of the kinds of plants that live in some of these biomes.

The Tundra and High Mountains

These are areas that remain frozen most of the year. They have six to 10 inches of precipitation each year. Summer may only be about 60 days long, and the average temperatures may only be 45 degrees Fahrenheit. During the summers, the top foot or so of soil may thaw. The frozen ground beneath will not absorb the melted snows or rains, so marshes and swamps are commonly found in the tundra. The plants of the tundra region are mostly mosses, low shrubs, and wildflowers. Plant varieties that grow close to the ground are able to survive the cold, dry winds that blow throughout the area. They are also able to take advantage of the protection offered by the thin snowfalls of the winter months.

Forests

Forests cover approximately one-third of the earth's surface. There are three basic kinds of forests: needleleaf, broadleaf, and tropical rain forests.

Needleleaf forests will usually have cold winters and cool summers. They often have very sandy soils. Most of the plants are **conifers** such as cedars, firs, hemlocks, pines, redwoods, and spruces. The forest floors may have ferns and mosses growing at the bases of the trees.

Broadleaf forests will also have cold winters, but they will have warm, wet summers. Most of the plants are **deciduous**. They will lose all of their leaves during the fall months and grow new leaves in the spring. Plants include basswoods, beeches, birches, chestnuts, elms, hickories, maples, oaks, poplars, tulip trees, and walnuts. Wildflowers, seedlings, and shrubs will abound on the forest floor.

Tropical rain forests have warm, wet weather all year. Most of the plants are broadleaf plants. Because of the year-round warm weather, these broadleaf plants will not all lose their leaves at the same time. Plants will include mahoganies and teaks. Few plants, other than ferns, are able to grow on the dark forest floor. Orchids and vines work their way up to the sunshine higher up in the forest.

Grasslands

Grasslands are open areas with mostly grasses in their natural state. Often grassland areas have been plowed up and are now being used for agriculture. Scientists identify three types of grasslands: steppes, prairies, and savannas.

Steppes are relatively dry areas. Plants consist mostly of short grasses.

Prairies are areas with more moisture. They may have hills, groups of trees, rivers, and streams in their midst. Plants consist mostly of taller grasses.

Savannas are dry in the winter months and wet in the summer months. Tall, stiff grasses are the dominant plants.

Deserts

Deserts cover about one-fifth of the earth's surface. Deserts have almost no plant life. They have very little rain and usually have very sandy or rocky soil. During at least some parts of the year, temperatures will reach more than 100 degrees Fahrenheit. Typical plants include cacti, creosote bushes, palm trees, sagebrush, yuccas, and wildflowers. These plants do not grow close to each other. Their roots spread out over large areas in an attempt to absorb as much water as possible. The succulent plants, such as the cacti, are adapted to hold water for as long as possible.

Aquatic

There are two kinds of aquatic biomes. **Freshwater biomes** include lakes, rivers, and ponds. **Saltwater biomes** include the oceans and seas. Plants in aquatic areas may grow near the surface to get as much sunlight as possible for photosynthesis. They are also found in shallow water areas and growing along the shorelines. Some plants, such as eelgrass, are able to grow completely underwater. Other plants, like duckweed, float freely along the surface of the water. Many other plants grow partly above the water and partly below the surface. Water marigolds are an example of this last kind of plant.

Activities:

1. Using magazines and catalogs, make a poster for each type of biome. Label the plants. Display your posters on a bulletin board.

2. Make up a series of flashcards using plant pictures. Have your students classify the plants according to their natural biomes.

Name_____ Date _____

For the Student:

Match the description in Column B with the correct term in Column A. Write the correct letter on the blank line.

Column A

_____ 1. Natural community

_____ 2. Biome

_____ 3. Tundra

_____ 4. Needleleaf forest

_____ 5. Broadleaf forest

_____ 6. Tropical rain forest

_____ 7. Steppe

_____ 8. Prairie

_____ 9. Savanna

_____ 10. Desert

_____ 11. Freshwater

_____ 12. Saltwater

Column B

A. Oceans

B. Weather, soil, plants, and animals

C. Lakes, rivers, and ponds

D. Units that have similar plants, animals, and climate

E. Area with cold winters, cool summers, and coniferous plants

F. Areas with dry winters, wet summers, and tall, stiff grasses

G. Areas that remain frozen most of the year

H. Areas with warm weather all year and broad-leaf plants

I. Areas with tall grasses

J. Areas with cold winters, warm summers, and deciduous plants

K. Areas with almost no plant life and very little rain

L. Dry areas with short grasses

What Good Are You, Anyway?
The Importance of Plants

You have learned just what a plant is. You have learned the parts of a plant. You should know how plants reproduce and where different kinds of plants are found. Let's think about why plants are important.

First of all, plants provide us with **food**. We eat many plants ourselves. Think about what you have eaten today. Did you have cereal for breakfast? Did you have a sandwich for lunch? Perhaps you will have an apple for a snack after school. We eat a lot of foods that come directly from plants. We eat almost every part of a plant. Corn, rice, and wheat are seeds. Beets and carrots are roots. Leaves that we might eat include spinach, lettuce, and cabbage. Celery and asparagus are stems, while broccoli and cauliflower are flowers. Finally, some of our favorites, like apples, bananas, and oranges, are fruits.

Sometimes we do not eat the plants directly, but we benefit from them. Many of us drink milk or eat products made with milk. Of course, the milk comes from a cow, but what does that cow depend on for food—plants. Without plants for the cow, we could not have a bowl of ice cream after supper.

Plants are important for other reasons as well. They provide us with very important **raw materials**. A raw material is a material that can be used to make something else. For example, trees provide us with wood. The wood can be cut up into lumber. The lumber can then be used to build our homes or to make the furniture we use inside our homes. Trees also provide us with wood chips. They can be used to make paper and paper products. Cork that we use as bottle stoppers or for bulletin boards comes from the bark of special trees. Natural rubber is a product from trees as well. Turpentine is made from the sap of certain pine trees. Many of our clothes are made with cotton. Cotton material is made with the fibers from cotton plants. Cotton is also used in making many towels, blankets, and carpets. Rope and twine are made from jute, hemp, or sisal plants.

For many years, people have depended on plants as **medicines**. Long ago, South American Indians used the bark from the cinchona tree to reduce fevers. It is still used today to make quinine, a medicine that is used to treat malaria. Digitalis is a medicine used to treat heart disease, and it comes from the purple foxglove flower. Some Mexican yam roots are used to make cortisone, a common drug used to treat arthritis and other diseases.

Plants provide us with food, clothing, shelter, and medicine. These are all very important to us if we want to have safe and healthy lives. Plants do more for us. They provide us with **beauty and pleasure**. They can also make our lives happier. Imagine the sight of cherry trees in bloom in Washington, D.C., in the spring. Thousands of people visit Washington each year just to see those beautiful, flowering trees. Imagine the smile of a young child who has just walked into the house and been greeted with the smell of a Christmas tree, set up and ready to be decorated. The memory of that smell may last for many years to come.

Plants provide us with many things. Without plants, we could not survive.

Name _____ Date _____

For the Student:

1. Give some examples of foods we eat from each of the following plant parts.

    a. seeds: _____

    b. roots: _____

    c. stems: _____

    d. leaves: _____

    e. fruit: _____

    f. flowers: _____

2. What are three raw materials that can come from trees?

_____

3. What can pine tree sap be used for?

_____

4. What plant is used when making a cotton t-shirt?

_____

5. When I get poison ivy, I need to have a cortisone shot. What plant helps me?

_____

6. What plants do you think are beautiful? Why?

_____

_____

7. What plant smells bring back happy memories for you? Why?

_____

_____

Activities:

1. Develop a plant food journal. Have the students record all the food that they have eaten for a certain period of time (one or two days). Develop two categories: primary plant food sources and secondary plant food sources. Classify the food that the students have eaten into the proper categories.
2. Inventory your classroom. Develop a list or photo journal of items that are made from plants. Create a newspaper or bulletin board to display your final results.
3. Research local industries. How many of them use plant products as raw materials? How many of them use plant products during the manufacturing process? Arrange for a visit to a local factory.
4. Plan a field trip to a local grocery store. Have students locate foods made from each of the parts of a plant. Assign students to different sections of the store: one group to frozen foods, another group to fresh fruits and vegetables, and another group to canned food. Compare the results.

Why Don't You Stop In for Dinner? Carnivorous Plants

You have learned that plants are producers. They make their own food using carbon dioxide, water, chlorophyll, and the sun's energy. Plants use their roots to get water and nutrients from the soil. Well, some plants grow in areas that have very poor soil. The soil does not have enough nutrients for the plants to grow properly. Some of the plants have found a special way to get the extra nutrients that they need. They eat insects! These are called **carnivorous plants**. (By the way, these plants still use photosynthesis to make their own food. They are just lucky to have two ways to get food!)

One kind of carnivorous plant is the pitcher plant. This plant has special, tube-shaped leaves. When it rains, the leaves gather up the water and hold on to it. These leaves also have tiny hairs, called **cilia**. The hairs all point downward, into the leaf and into the water. When an unsuspecting insect happens to land on the leaf of a pitcher plant, it is in trouble. The insect cannot move up the leaf against all the cilia. It may stuggle for a while, but then it will get tired and slip down the leaf. It will land in the water that has been stored in the leaf, and the poor insect will drown. Special fluids in the leaf of the plant will then digest the insect, and the plant will get the extra nutrients it needs.

Another kind of carnivorous plant is called the sundew plant. A sundew plant's leaves also have tiny hairs or cilia on them. This time the hairs are sticky. When an unlucky insect

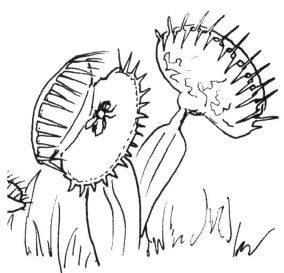

lands on one of these leaves, it cannot get away. The hairs will eventually wrap around the insect. More sticky fluid is secreted onto the insect, and it finally cannot breathe. It suffocates. The leaf fluids will digest the insect, and the nutrients not provided by the soil are available to the plant.

The final kind of carnivorous plant is a Venus' flytrap. This kind of plant has leaves with hinges, like a door. The leaves are also covered with sensitive hairs. When the hairs feel an insect land on a leaf, the hinges quickly close. There are bristly hairs at the end of each leaf. When the hinge closes, the bristles lock together. The insect is trapped inside the closed leaf. The plant uses special fluids to digest the insect, and then the leaf will open up again, ready for the next meal.

Luckily for us, these plants are small and only feed on insects. For now, we are safe and do not have to worry about people-eating plants, except in the movies!

Name _____ Date _____

For the Student:

1. What does the word *carnivorous* mean?

_____

_____

2. How are carnivorous plants different from other plants?

_____

_____

3. What are three types of carnivorous plants?

_____

_____

4. What do all three of them have on their leaves?

_____

_____

5. Why do these plants need to digest insects?

_____

_____

6. What might happen if a Pitcher Plant tried to grow in an area without any rain?

_____

_____

7. These carnivorous plants do not have mouths. How can they "eat" the insects?

_____

_____

Activities:

Assign some creative writing assignments.

From an insect's perspective:
1. A grieving child describing how his or her parent died, eaten by a carnivorous plant.
2. A coroner's report of an autopsy of an insect eaten by a carnivorous plant.
3. A missing insect report filed.
4. An inspector's report detailing the crime scene.

From a plant's point of view:
5. An explanation of why it ate an insect.
6. A detailed account of the process of eating an insect.
7. A parent plant teaching a child plant how to trap and eat an insect.

Answer Keys

Introduction (page 2)
Answers will vary.

A Plant by Any Other Name (page 5)
1. Organisms reproduce, grow, develop, use energy, need food, and are made of cells.
2. Yes, plants have all six features of life.
3. No, plants are multicellular organisms.
4. The nucleus controls the life activities of the plant's cells.
5. Plant cells have organelles that help the nuclei perform their duties.
6. A plant is a multicellular organism that contains a nucleus and cell walls as well as organelles, which allow it to carry on life processes as a producer.

Kings Play Cards On Fridays, Generally Speaking: Classifying Organisms (page 7)
1. Kingdom, Phylum, Class, Order, Family, Genus, Species
2. The largest group of plants is called the plant kingdom.
3. Bryophytes and Tracheophytes are the two major phyla of plants.
4. Vascular plants have tube-like structures that move water and food to different parts of the plants. Nonvascular plants do not have the tube-like structures.
5. They do not have tubes for carrying water, so they must be close to water to survive.

A Class Act (page 10)
1. F; five kingdoms
2. F; some plants
3. T
4. T
5. F; with spores
6. F; smaller than ferns
7. F; moist areas
8. T
9. F; inside of cones
10. T
11. F; a coniferous plant
12. T
13. T
14. T
15. F; a gymnosperm

Parts of a Plant Cell (page 13)
1. A plant cell is the smallest part of a plant.
2a. It supports and protects the cell.
b. It stores cell sap.
c. It aids with photosynthesis.

d. It aids with respiration.
e. It controls all cell activities.
3. Animal cells do not have cell walls or vacuoles.
4. They both have protoplasts, mitochondria, and a nucleus.

Getting to the Root of the Problem (page 15)
1. The roots, stem, and leaves are the vegetative matter.
2. They anchor the plant, absorb water and minerals, and store food.
3. Two basic kinds of roots are fibrous roots and taproots.
4. Primary roots grow out of seeds, and secondary roots branch out of primary roots.
5. The root cap protects the tip of the root as it moves through the soil.
6. They need to absorb lots of water and minerals.
7. Roots grow down with the force of gravity.
8. Roots grow toward water.

Root Activities (pages 16–17)
Demonstrating that roots take water from the soil for plants:
1. No, one plant will be wilted while the other one is healthy.
2. Yes, they wither and die without water.
3. They absorb water through their roots.
Demonstrating that roots anchor a plant:
1. No, the radish without roots falls over.
2. The roots hold a plant in the soil.
Demonstrating that gravity affects root growth:
1. They all grew down.
2. They all grew up.
3. Gravity caused the roots to grow down.

What's Holding Things Up? Stems (page 20)
1. Stems hold up the leaves and separate them, they store food and water, and they move food and water between the roots and leaves.
2. Xylem tissue moves water from the roots to the other parts of the plant.
3. Phloem tissue moves food from the leaves to the other parts of the plant.
4. Cambium is growth tissue that makes new xylem and phloem.
5. Herbaceous stems are soft, smooth, and green, while woody stems are rough, stiff, and brown.
6. It is a stem that grows above the ground.
7. It is a stem that grows along the ground and may form new plants.
8. It is a stem that grows under the ground.
9. A potato is one example of a tuber.

10. They have tendrils that allow them to hold on to other structures and grow up toward the sunlight.

The Fast Food Industry: "Leaf" It to Me (page 25)
1. make food
2. blade, petiole
3. evaporation
4. palisade, spongy
5. stomata
6. daylight, darkness, temperature
7. carbon dioxide, oxygen
8. transpiration
9. one
10. petiole
11. parallel
12. net-veined
13. pinnately
14. palmately
15. other side
16. level
17. winds
18. precipitation/rain
19. water
20. absorb, hold

Leaf Activities (pages 26–27)
Observing the functions of leaves:
1A. The substance was water.
B. It evaporated from the leaves of the plant.
2A. One plant will die, while the other one should thrive.
B. Leaves are needed to produce food for the plant.
3A. One plant will thrive (B), while the other plant withers (A).
B. The stomata were covered on the dying plant so it could not get the carbon dioxide it needed to make food.
4A. It turned white (lime water) or yellow (Bromothymol blue).
B. The gas released was oxygen.

A Rose by Any Other Name: Flowers
Diagram (page 31)
1. anther	6. calyx (sepal)
2. stigma	7. pistil
3. corolla (petals)	8. style
4. filament	9. ovary
5. stamen	

Matching (page 32)
1. B	6. G
2. C	7. I
3. H	8. J
4. F	9. E
5. A	10. D

Starting Over: Seeds
Diagram (page 35)
1. embryo
2. radicle
3. hypocotyl
4. cotyledon
5. epicotyl
6. seed coat
7. endosperm

Questions (page 36)
1. They contain the young plant that allows the plant to reproduce.
2. Answers will vary.
3. No, redwood seeds are only one-sixteenth of an inch, but they become the tallest trees in the world.
4. It has naked seeds because a hemlock is a cone-bearing plant.
5. Fleshy fruit, dry fruit, and aggregate fruit are three kinds of ovaries.
6. The seed coat protects the seed.
7. They form the embryo.
8. It stores food for the cotyledons and embryo.

Gone With the Wind: Seed Dispersal (page 38)
1. Plants need water, minerals, and sunlight.
2. Some of them will not survive.
3. *Dispersal* means "carrying away."
4. Wind, water, and wild animals can disperse seeds.
5. Seeds get stuck on their clothes or they pick seeds and carry them to another area.
6. Seeds are carried to areas where there is less competition and a better chance for survival.

All Organisms Reproduce: Sexual Reproduction (page 42)
1. Plants reproduce through sexual and asexual reproduction.
2. Flowering plants, cone-bearing plants, ferns, and mosses are capable of sexual reproduction.
3. The stamens are the male parts and the pistil is the female part of a flower.
4. Pollination is the process of transferring pollen grains from the stamens to the pistil.
5. Wind, insects, and birds help in pollination.
6. The plants do not have wind as a pollinator, so they depend more on insects and birds.
7. They want to attract insects and birds because they are cross-pollinating plants. The pollen must travel from one plant to another.
8. Fertilization is the process of joining the male cell and the female cell.
9. One kind of cone has the male cells, and the other kind of cone has the female cells.
10. Ferns and mosses go through this cycle.

All Organisms Reproduce: Asexual Reproduction (page 45)
1. A cactus can reproduce by budding.
2. Cut the old potato into pieces, including some potato and at least one eye in each piece. Plant the pieces.
3. It is a piece of stem growing along the ground.
4. Strawberries and grass reproduce with runners. (Also, ferns, irises, and blueberry plants)
5. Anchor the tips of branches near the ground where roots can form.
6. Answers will vary.
7. D
8. F
9. A
10. E
11. C
12. B

Germination of Plants (page 47)
1. Germination is the early growth of a plant from a seed.
2. Proper temperature, enough moisture, and oxygen are needed for germination.
3. They are growing in colder climates and need to germinate earlier to have a full growing season before the cold weather sets in again.
4. Seeds get moisture from the ground.
5. It may take a long time to germinate or it may not germinate at all.
6. It may rot before it germinates.
7. Oxygen is a part of the many changes that take place when a seed is becoming a new plant.
8. It becomes the main root, anchors the seed, and provides water and minerals to the embryo.
9. It becomes the upper part of the plant and contains the first leaves.
10. They must know about germination, seeds, air and soil temperature, the amount of moisture in the soil, when to plant, the weather, the soil, and the kinds of seeds to plant.

Photosynthesis and Respiration (page 51)
1. Photosynthesis is the process plants use to make their own food. Respiration is the process plants use to release energy.
2. Photosynthesis requires carbon dioxide and water. Respiration requires sugar and oxygen.
3. Carbon dioxide comes from the air, and the water comes from the soil. The sugar is from the plant's own food, and the oxygen comes from the air.
4. They trap the Sun's energy using chlorophyll.
5. Sugar and oxygen are made in photosynthesis. Carbon dioxide and water are produced during respiration.

6. They use the sugar to build and repair the plant's cells, tissues, and organs and to make cellulose for cell walls.
7. It is released into the air for animals to breathe.
8. They don't have green leaves with chlorophyll.
9. They photosynthesize the most during the summer, when the days are the longest and they have the most sunshine.
10. The products made during photosynthesis are used for respiration, and the products made during respiration are used for photosynthesis.

Habitats of Plants (page 54)
1. B   7. L
2. D   8. I
3. G   9. F
4. E   10. K
5. J   11. C
6. H   12. A

The Importance of Plants (page 56)
1. Answers will vary.
2. Raw materials that come from trees include lumber, wood chips, cork, natural rubber, and pine sap (any three).
3. Pine tree sap is used to make turpentine.
4. Cotton fibers from the cotton plant are used to make a cotton t-shirt.
5. The Mexican yam plant is the source of cortisone.
6. Answers will vary.
7. Answers will vary.

Carnivorous Plants (page 58)
1. *Carnivorous* means "meat eating."
2. They get their food by photosynthesis *and* by eating insects.
3. The pitcher plant, sundew plant, and the Venus' flytrap are carnivorous plants.
4. Tiny hairs or cilia are on their leaves.
5. The soil where they grow does not have enough nutrients.
6. It would not be able to drown the insects and would not get enough nutrients. It might die.
7. Special fluids in their leaves digest the insects. The nutrients are absorbed into the leaves through the stomata.

Bibliography

Bresler, Lynn. *The Usborne Book of Earth Facts.* Tulsa, Oklahoma: EDC Publishing, 1986.

Cadice, Richard and Ortleb, Edward. *Plants.* St. Louis, Missouri: Milliken Publishing Company, 1968.

Cartwright, Mary. *Protecting Our World.* Tulsa, Oklahoma: EDC Publishing, 1991.

Friedland, Mary K. *Green Plants: Life Science in Action.* Hayward, California: Janus Book Publishers, 1982.

Gottlieb, Joan S. *The Wonders of Science: Plant Life.* Austin, Texas: Steck-Vaughn Company, 1986.

Heimler, Charles H. *Focus on Life Science.* Columbus, Ohio: Merrill Publishing Company, 1981.

Heimler, Charles H. *Principles of Science: Book One.* Columbus, Ohio: Merrill Publishing Company, 1986.

Microsoft. *Encarta '95: The Complete Interactive Multimedia Encyclopedia.*

Plant Science Manual. Oaklawn, Illinois: Ideal School Supply Co.

World Book Encyclopedia. Chicago, Illinois; Scott Fetzer Company, 1988.